Christmas Lights

By Valerie Howard

Cast of Characters:

Bobby Gardner- older boy without a lot of money (12 lines)

Mrs. Rachel Gardner- single mother (5 lines)

Sarah Oliver- spoiled girl (11 lines)

Ruby Oliver- proper girl (9 lines)

Mr. James Oliver- rich and uppity father (10 lines)

Mrs. Pamela Oliver- rich and uppity mother (2 lines)

Katrina Champion- sporty girl (8 lines)

Brady Champion- boy, wears army clothing (7 lines)

Col. Stanley Champion- ex-military father (7 lines)

Mrs. Miranda Champion- soccer coach mother (2 lines)

Lilly Smith- younger girl (8 lines)

Brian Smith- older boy (7 lines)

Mr. Daniel Smith- Christian father (10 lines)

Mrs. Emily Smith- Christian mother (8 lines)

Contest Judge (3 lines)

Neighborhood kids- sing and help decorate (No lines)

Scene I

Enter all kids, waving behind them saying, "Have a good vacation!" "See you next year!" and walking across the stage carrying/wearing backpacks.

Sing <u>Joy to the World</u> by Isaac Watts

Joy to the world! The Lord is come;
Let earth receive her King;
Let every heart prepare him room.
And heav'n and nature sing, and heav'n and nature sing,
And heav'n and heav'n and nature sing.

Joy to the earth! The Savoir reigns;
Let men their songs employ;
While fields and floods, rocks, hills and plains
Repeat the sounding joy, repeat the sounding joy,
Repeat, repeat the sounding joy.

No more let sins and sorrows grow,
Nor thorns infest the ground;
He comes to make His blessings flow
Far as the curse is found, far as the curse is found,
Far as, far as the curse is found.

He rules the world with truth and grace,
And makes the nations prove
The glories of His righteousness,
And wonders of His love, and wonders of His love,
And wonders, wonders of His love.

Sarah: Guess what! *My* daddy bought us a snowman that lights up and spins around all by itself on the roof. He says that is what is going to make us win the neighborhood house-decorating contest for the fifth year in a row!

Katrina: Yeah? Well you've only won that many times because we weren't here last year. Our family has been getting up at—

Brady: (*Bragging*) Zero four hundred every morning and planning how we are going to decorate our house, so that prize money and trophy are going to be ours this year!

Lilly: How much money do you win for having the prettiest house?

Ruby: Well, it's only five hundred dollars. Not much, really, but mother and father let Sarah and I split it every year and buy whatever we want on our trips overseas.

Brian: So, Bobby, how are you and your mom going to decorate your house this year?

Bobby: I don't know. If you ask me, the whole thing is a stupid idea. I don't care too much about stringing up lights and spinning snowmen and all. Anyway, Mom is too busy with her job. She doesn't have time to decorate the house for a dumb contest.

Sarah: Well, I wouldn't bother Bobby with stuff like that, Brian. Neither of you would win anyway…you never do.

Bobby: Maybe this year will be different, Sarah. Just you wait and see.

Ruby: Well, may the best family win. See you at the judging ceremony! *(Tries to shake Bobby's hand, but Bobby ignores it and goes inside his house)*

The rest of the kids shrug and go inside.
Lights out.

Scene II

Ruby, Sarah, and Mr. Oliver out on their lawn, a small ladder is on the side of their house, boxes of decorations in front of their house..

Ruby: We are so glad that you are letting us help you decorate the house this year, father!

Sarah: Yeah, do you think we're going to win again?

Mr. Oliver: Of *course* we'll win, princess. (*Calling inside*). Pamela, have you seen the light up angel I had on the house last year? I thought I put it out on the lawn last night with all the other decorations, but it's not here.

Mrs. Oliver (*From inside the house*): No, dear, I thought you got rid of that because the light was broken.

Mr. Oliver: No, I had Dan fix it…Never mind, I must have been thinking about something else. (*To the kids*). Okay, kids, now I'm going to be up on the roof, so Sarah, you find whatever I need, and Ruby, you bring it up to me on the ladder, got it?

Sarah and Ruby (*Together*): Yes, Daddy/Yes, Father.

Mr. Oliver: Okay, now darling, find the snowflake lights and give them to Ruby.

Sarah looks through all the boxes while Mr. Oliver climbs the ladder and Ruby waits impatiently.

Sarah: I can't find them, Daddy, they're not in any of these boxes.

Mr. Oliver: That's all right. They must be in the garage. Get me the colored lights then, I'll start with those.

Sarah gets a string of lights and hands them to Ruby who brings them up a few steps of the ladder.

The three mime decorating the house. Ruby comes back and forth from the "lawn" to the stepladder, bringing supplies occasionally.

Enter Mrs. Champion, blowing whistle. Katrina and Brady follow with lights wound around both their arms, jogging.

Mrs. Champion: Move, move, move! Lights on at zero seven hundred, window painting at zero eight hundred… move it, move it!

Enter Mr. Champion with clipboard and a pen, a whistle around his neck.

Mr. Champion: Status report of the inflatable Christmas tree ASAP!

Mrs. Champion: It is in the garage, sir!

Mr. Champion: Negative. I just checked there. Katrina, Brady, status of the inflatable Christmas tree.

Katrina and Brady (*At attention and saluting*): We don't know, sir!

Mr. Champion: At ease, children. We'll find it. I think I saw a box marked Christmas decorations in the attic. Brady, go check, son.

Brady: Yes, sir! (*Runs into house*).

Mr. Champion: The rest of you, get back to decorating. We will win this competition, or my name isn't Colonel Stanley Champion!

Champions mime decorating their house. Olivers are still decorating. Brady comes back out and joins the Champions and shrugs to his father. They all continue to decorate.

Enter Mr. and Mrs. Smith with Lilly and Brian from inside their house, each one carrying a box full of decorations.

Mrs. Smith: Isn't it fun to decorate the house as a family?

Lilly: Yeah! Can we put up the popcorn string I made at school?

Mr. Smith: Sure, honey! I bet we can find a perfect spot for it!

Brian: I think it would look good right above the door! And we could put the wreath *on* the door and the lights around the windows and the window stickers *on* the windows and then—

Mr. Smith: Whoa, whoa, slow down, Brian. We have all day to figure that stuff out. Why don't we start by getting the wreath on the door and go from there?

Mrs. Smith: Good idea. I remember seeing it in this box yesterday. (*Searches through the box without finding it*) Hmm… maybe it was in a different box. (*Searches all the boxes without finding it*) Well, maybe there's another box inside.

Brian: These are all the boxes, Mom. There were only four of them.

Mr. Smith: I wouldn't worry about it. I'm sure it's somewhere. Let's start with that popcorn string then, shall we Lilly?

Lilly: Yay!

All families mime decorating their houses while singing.

Sing <u>Deck the Halls</u> by John Ceiriog Hughes

Deck the halls with boughs of holly,
Fa la la la la la la la la.
'Tis the season to be jolly,
Fa la la la la la la la la.
Don we now our gay apparel,
Fa la la la la la la la la.
Troll the ancient Christmas carol,
Fa la la la la la la la la.
See the blazing yule before us,
Fa la la la la la la la la.
Strike the harp and join the chorus.
Fa la la la la la la la la.
Follow me in merry measure,
Fa la la la la la la la la.
While I tell of Christmas treasure,
Fa la la la la la la la la.

Mr. Oliver (*Calling over to Mr. Smith*): Hey, Dan, do you remember that light up angel decoration you fixed for me last year?

Mr. Smith: Um, yeah. You mean the one that just needed the light bulb replaced?

Mr. Oliver: Yes, well, it seems to be missing from amongst my decorations. Did you forget to give it back to me?

Mr. Smith: I don't think so. These are all the decorations we have, and it's not in any of these boxes.

Mr. Oliver (*Getting irritated*): Well, I'm *sure* you still have it, because I am *very* organized, unlike *some* people, and I would never misplace my prize winning decoration.

Mr. Smith: James, I'm sure I gave it back to you. Please don't get upset.

12

Mr. Oliver: Don't tell me what to do! If one of my neighbors is being dishonest, then I am going to get upset! I'll go into your garage and attic and search them for myself if I have to!

Mr. Smith: Please, that won't be necessary. I'll send Brian and Lilly to check right now. (*To children*). Kids, please go try to find Mr. Oliver's gigantic light up angel in the house and garage.

Brian and Lilly run inside the house.

Mr. Champion (*Calling after children*): And while you're at it, look for my inflatable Christmas tree! That's missing too!

Mrs. Smith: Now, Stan, I know we don't have your Christmas tree. You just moved here a few months ago. It's probably still packed away in a box somewhere.

Brady: No, it's not. We searched the whole house. It's not there.

Katrina: But Sarah and Ruby have one just like it on their lawn!

Ruby: This one is ours. We've had it forever!

Sarah: Yeah, we don't *lose* our Christmas decorations like *some* people!

Brady: Well we don't *steal* Christmas decorations like *some* people!

Mr. Oliver: Now that's quite enough. The Oliver family has a good reputation in this community and I will not have you two calling us common thieves.

Mr. Champion: Don't talk to my children that way, and that's an order!

An argument breaks out, Brian and Lilly return, all mothers come out and join in, kids in each other's faces, waving arms and arguing. Mr. and Mrs. Smith are not yelling at anyone, but trying to calm people down.

Mr. Smith (*Raises hands up in the air*): WAIT! (*Fighting stops*). Okay, I think I know what's going on here. The Oliver family is missing a light up angel, the Champion family is missing a huge blow up Christmas tree, and our family is missing our front door wreath. (*Everyone nods*). Obviously, we have some sort of rodent problem, like a raccoon or something that got into our garages and carried away some of our decorations.

Mr. Oliver: Finally, someone is talking some sense around here!

Mr. Smith: Let's all just forget about it, take the day off from decorating, and start again tomorrow when we've all cooled down and can concentrate on the contest, okay?

Everyone agrees and picks up their boxes and goes inside.
Lights fade.

Scene III

Bobby and his mother enter and talk sadly.

Mrs. Gardner: I know it's the day before Christmas Eve, honey, but I have to go out and look for another job. Things have just been so tight since I lost that job at the diner last month. I know you were hoping for a bike for Christmas, but we will just have to buy Christmas presents in a few months when we can afford them, okay?

Bobby (*Obviously devastated*): But, Mom, it's *Christmas*! How can we have no presents on Christmas?

Mrs. Gardner: I'm so sorry honey, but I really have to go. Be good and take care of yourself.

Mrs. Gardner exits.

Bobby (*To himself*): Well, maybe I can win that five hundred dollars if I can take a few more unwanted decorations off people's hands. *(He grabs a box from behind the house and starts going through it).*

Enter Katrina, Brady, Sarah, Ruby, Brian, and Lilly.

Lilly: Hey Bobby, whatcha doin'?

Bobby (*Quickly putting the decorations back*): Nothing. Just thinking about decorating my house for the contest.

Katrina: Yeah, we were all doing that too, but we all had decorations missing, so our parents wanted us to go around and see if anyone had seen our stuff.

Ruby: The contest is tomorrow night and now we're missing all of our white lights!

Lilly: Are you missing anything Bobby?

Bobby: Umm, yeah, now that you mention it, we haven't been able to find our… umm…our…

Sarah: I didn't think you had any decorations. You never decorate your house for the contest.

Bobby: Well, we got some this year.

Brady: Yeah? Let me see 'em. *(Pushes Bobby aside and all the kids start looking through the box).*

Katrina: That looks just like our blow up Christmas tree!

Ruby: And that's our light up angel!

Lilly: And that's the wreath Mommy made!

Brian: Bobby, where did you find all this? It's all our missing decorations!

Katrina: He didn't find it, Brian. He stole it all in the first place!

Sarah (*Gasps*): You thief! I bet you were trying to sabotage the contest for all of us and win yourself!

All Kids (*Speaking to Bobby angrily*): How could you? That's our stuff! Why would you steal all of our decorations? I thought you were our friend!

Bobby (*Holding his hands up to silence everyone*): Okay, okay! Your families have so many nice decorations, and we don't have any, I didn't think you would notice one or two things missing when you all had so much. But, fine! Just take them back! I don't care!

Bobby runs into his house, leaving the kids on the stage in stunned silence for a moment.

Enter Mrs. Smith.

Mrs. Smith: Was that Bobby you were talking to?

Katrina: Yeah, what a loser!

Mrs. Smith: Be easy on him, Katrina. Bobby's mom lost her job last month. She told me last week that she doesn't even have money to buy Bobby any presents for Christmas. Poor kid. (*Shakes her head as she looks at Bobby's house*). I'm going to pick up a few things at the store, kids, Dad's home if you need anything. Have fun decorating!

Mrs. Smith exits the stage.

Brian: Wow…I can't imagine not having any presents on Christmas.

Sarah: Or any decorations to decorate your house with for the contest.

Katrina: Poor Bobby! I know he shouldn't have stolen all our stuff, but he should have told us that he needed help, and we would have done something for him!

Kids pause, thinking and looking down at their shoes.

Lilly (*Points her finger in the air*): We can still decorate his house for him!

Ruby: That's a good idea, Lilly! We already have a bunch of decorations right here!

Kids decorate Bobby's house.

Sing <u>Away in a Manger</u> by John Thomas McFarland

Away in a manger, no crib for a bed,
The little Lord Jesus laid down His sweet head;
The stars in the sky looked down where He lay,
The little Lord Jesus asleep on the hay.

The cattle are lowing, the baby awakes,
But little Lord Jesus, no crying He makes.
I love Thee, Lord Jesus, look down from the sky,
And stay by my cradle till morning is nigh.

Be near me, Lord Jesus, I ask Thee to stay
Close by me forever, and love me, I pray.
Bless all the dear children in Thy tender care,
And fit us for heaven, to live with Thee there.

Enter all parents (but Mrs. Gardner) after kids are done decorating and singing.

Mrs. Oliver: Kids, what on earth are you doing?

Sarah: We're decorating Bobby's house, Mommy.

Mr. Champion: But those are all our decorations!

Brady: We know. Bobby and his mom don't have any decorations, so we are letting him borrow some of ours!

Mrs. Smith *(With shopping bags)*: Children, that is so sweet of you!

Lilly: But Bobby still won't have any presents on Christmas. His mom said they don't have any money for presents right now.

Mrs. Smith: Children, I have an idea. Follow me!

Kids follow Mrs. Smith into her house. Adults go into their respective houses. Lights out.

18

Scene IV

Lights up.
Gardner house is decorated. A few decorations are on the other houses.

Enter all parents and kids out of their houses (except Bobby and Mrs. Gardner) go to the Gardner's house with presents behind their backs.

Parents and kids all gather outside Gardner's house to sing carols.
Mrs. Gardner and Bobby come to the door and listen.

Sing <u>Silent Night</u> by Joseph Mohr (translated by J. F. Young)

Silent night, holy night, all is calm, all is bright
'Round yon virgin mother and child.
Holy infant so tender and mild,
Sleep in heavenly peace,
Sleep in heavenly peace.

Silent night, holy night, shepherds quake at the sight.
Glories stream from heaven afar,
Heavenly hosts sing Alleluia;
Christ the Savior is born!
Christ the Savior is born!

Silent night, holy night, Son of God, love's pure light
Radiant beams from Thy holy face,
With the dawn of redeeming grace,
Jesus, Lord at Thy birth,
Jesus, Lord at Thy birth.

Sing <u>Hark the Herald Angels Sing</u> by Charles Wesley

Hark! The herald angels sing,
"Glory to the newborn King;
Peace on earth, and mercy mild,
God and sinners reconciled!"
Joyful all ye nations rise,
Join the triumph of the skies;
With th'angelic voice proclaim,
"Christ is born in Bethlehem!"
Hark! The herald angels sing.
"Glory to the newborn King."

Christ, by highest heav'n adored;
Christ, the everlasting Lord!
Late in time behold Him come,
Offspring of the virgin's womb:
Veiled in flesh the Godhead see;
Hail the'incarnate Deity,
Pleased as man with men to dwell,
Jesus, our Emmanuel.
Hark! The herald angels sing.
"Glory to the newborn King."

Hail the heav'n born Prince of Peace!
Hail the Sun of Righteousness!
Light and life to all He brings,
Ris'n with healing in His wings.
Mild He lays His glory by,
Born that man no more may die,
Born to raise the sons of earth,
Born to give them second birth.
Hark! The herald angels sing.
"Glory to the newborn King."

Everyone (*Handing gifts to Bobby*): Merry Christmas!

Mrs. Gardner: Thank you all! You are the best neighbors anyone could ask for! You decorated our house beautifully, and now these presents— I just don't know what to say!

Bobby: Why would you do all this for me, after I stole your decorations from you?

Brian: Well, Bobby, it's kind of like what happened on the very first Christmas.

Bobby: What do you mean?

Brian: On the first Christmas, God gave us a free gift— His only Son Jesus Christ. Jesus was born to live a perfect life and die on the cross to pay for our sins. Even though we were sinners and did wrong things against God, He still gave us Jesus. Just like we're giving you gifts today, even after what you did to us.

Mr. Smith: That's right, Brian. The Bible says that, "God showed his love toward us, in that, while we were yet sinners, Christ died for us." He gave us Jesus to die for our sins when we deserved to die for our own sins. That's the true spirit of Christmas— showing others grace just as God did on that first Christmas so long ago.

Bobby: Thank you all for your gifts, and more importantly, for your forgiveness.

Enter Judge with a clipboard, trophy, and $500 check.

Judge: Well, everyone, I've made my final decision on this year's winner for the neighborhood house-decorating contest.

Sarah: Oh, no! We were so busy getting presents for Bobby and wrapping them that we forgot all about finishing our house decorations!

Ruby: It's okay, Sarah. We win every year. Why not let someone else have a chance this year?

Judge: And the winner is…the Gardner family!

Everyone cheers.

Judge: Here is your trophy and your check for five hundred dollars! Beautiful decorations this year Mrs. Gardner!

Mrs. Gardner (*Wiping away tears*): Thank you! Thank you all so very much!

Mrs. Smith: We are going around the neighborhood caroling. Would you two care to join us? We could use a few extra voices!

Bobby and Mrs. Gardner: We would love to!

Everyone turns to the audience.

Sing <u>We Wish You a Merry Christmas</u> by Unknown Author

We wish you a Merry Christmas
We wish you a Merry Christmas
We wish you a Merry Christmas
And a Happy New Year.
(Repeat)

Good tidings we bring
To you and your king
Good tidings for Christmas
And a happy new year.

We wish you a Merry Christmas
We wish you a Merry Christmas
We wish you a Merry Christmas
And a Happy New Year.
(Repeat)

Good tidings we bring.
To you and your king
Good tidings for Christmas
And a happy new year.

We wish you a Merry Christmas
We wish you a Merry Christmas
We wish you a Merry Christmas
And a Happy New Year.

We wish you a Merry Christmas
And a Happy New Year.

Everyone bows.
Lights out.

Props:

- Four cardboard houses with working doors

- Christmas lights

- Gym whistles

- Backpacks

- Purses

- Shopping bags

- Christmas decorations

- Popcorn string

- Boxes

- Stepladder

- Large $500 check

- Trophy

- Clipboards and pens

- Wrapped presents

Costumes:

All scenes take place outside, so scarves, hats, and boots or shoes would be appropriate costumes for all characters.

Set:

Four houses in this order from left to right: Gardner, Oliver, Smith, Champion. The Olivers should have a large "inflatable" Christmas tree painted on the outside of their house or an actual inflatable tree in front of their house. All house doors should be able to open and close to allow cast members to enter and exit through them. Mailboxes with the family names may also be helpful.

Variations:

For fewer characters:

- Mrs. Champion's lines may be called out from off-stage.

- Mrs. Oliver's first line may be called out from off-stage, and the second line given to Mr. Oliver.

For additional characters:

- A child character may be added to each family, giving a few lines of each other "sibling" to him/her.

- A panel of judges, instead of a singular judge, could be constructed, giving one line to each judge.

If you enjoyed this play, you might also like ...

Christmas Gifts by Valerie Howard

No Time For Christmas by Valerie Howard

Christmas Catastrophe by Steve and Valerie Howard

The Worst Christmas Ever by Elizabeth Rowe and Juliet Rowe

Find books for children, teens, and adults at
www.AuthorValerieHoward.com

Follow what's new at
www.Facebook.com/ValerieHowardBooks

Made in United States
North Haven, CT
02 September 2022